This Common
Uncommon

Rae Howells is a poet, journalist, academic and lavender farmer from Swansea. Her debut collection, *The language of bees*, was shortlisted for Wales Book of the Year. She has previously won both the Rialto Nature and Place and Welsh International poetry competitions and featured in journals including *Magma*, *The Rialto*, *Poetry Wales*, *New Welsh Review*, *Acumen* and *Poetry Ireland*. A keen environmentalist and a believer in the restorative power of wild places, she is poet in residence at Llanelli Wetland Centre. *This Common Uncommon* is her second poetry collection.

raehowells.co.uk

This Common Uncommon

Rae Howells

PARTHIAN

Parthian, Cardigan SA43 1ED
www.parthianbooks.com
First published in 2024
© Rae Howells 2024
ISBN 978-1-914595-90-5
Editor: Susie Wildsmith
Cover image: 'Clouds Beckon a Heathland Way – West Cross Common, Swansea', 2023, oil paints on board (16" x 20") by Mike Crafer
Cover design by Emily Courdelle
Typeset by Elaine Sharples
Printed and bound by 4edge Limited, UK
Published with the financial support of the Books Council of Wales
British Library Cataloguing in Publication Data
A cataloguing record for this book is available from the British Library
Printed on FSC accredited paper

For my daughters, Gwennan and Mabli

The law locks up the man or woman
Who steals the goose from off the common
But leaves the greater felon loose
Who steals the common from the goose.

The law demands that we atone
When we take things we do not own
But leaves the lords and ladies fine
Who take things that are yours or mine.
                                        – 18th C, trad.

CONTENTS

As are the changes of the green / So is the life of man

Sweet it was to mark the flower

Notes
Acknowledgements

Introduction

I first became aware of West Cross Common in 2020, during lockdown. We had hardly noticed it before, this overgrown brambly place on the edge of the estate. But when the pandemic hit and we were all confined to our houses – apart from that mandated daily walk – it became our family's go-to place. My husband, Phil, and I were both working from home, and with our two daughters still in primary school, we were in that hideous home-schooling frenzy of trying to juggle work with online meetings, lessons, worksheets and Joe Wicks fitness videos. We had more screen time than any of us could bear. The four of us (and Hazel the dog) were more than glad to escape the house and get outdoors.

First we assumed the only part we could access was a single path, running from the corner of Mulberry Avenue and Chestnut Avenue, almost parallel with Mulberry, leading up to the greater Clyne common and a splendid walk across the golf course. But once we were brave enough to head 'off piste' we found several minor paths which took us into the unknown, a maze of little glades, streams and copses.

Gradually we learned to spot where foxes had carved pathways through the bracken. We had fun following in their footsteps all the way across the common to Eastmoor Lane, to the fence with the rickety stile, and beyond that even more commons, some grazed by ponies or a mix of ponies and sheep, and studded in places with clear, still frog ponds, reflecting the sky.

In the absence of noisy traffic, birdsong suddenly seemed much louder, forcing us to notice. Limited to the places we could only get to on foot, we became more grounded, more present. Instead of looking outward, and with a destination in mind, we began to look around, and down, noticing details and plants and trees. We had no particular place to be, so meandered in circuits and loops, not line-shaped journeys with pre-determined endpoints.

We walked streets we'd never walked before, carved out new routes, got out our phones to learn more about the wildflowers, discovered the names of the birds we could suddenly hear so clearly.

This unremarkable suburb on the edge of Swansea became more than just 'the place we live': the houses, streets, shops, school, doctor's surgery. It was suddenly obvious that it was home to a thrumming, lively ecosystem. We began to see through animal eyes. West Cross Common was not a scrubby little waste ground at all, but a vital link in a long green chain that stretched from the very tip of the Gower Peninsula, across a network of interconnected commons, hedgerows, woodlands and rural land, until it reached the sliver of ancient woodland and the Washing House Brook that runs down the valley to the sea.

Naively, we assumed that this wild and green place would always be here. Surely a common was sacrosanct: not at threat from development. But we were wrong. With hindsight perhaps we should have foreseen how vulnerable it was, for several reasons:

- The land borders 'the settlement' (a planning term for the sprawl of our houses and streets), and thanks to new planning policies any land adjacent to the existing settlement can now be considered for affordable housing schemes.[1]
- It is owned by the Duke of Beaufort's estate, the Somerset Trust, major landowners in the UK who own vast swathes of the country, and are known to be robust in monetising their land.[2]
- It has some spectacular sea views, too – who wouldn't want to see those out of their windows?
- This section of the common is no longer utilised by the Gower Commoners for grazing, having been cut off from the rest of the common by a main road and a series of fences. Years of resulting neglect have seen its rare flowers and bog plants shaded under a bracken tide, and this kind of boggy landscape has itself been passed over as a habitat of value until very recently.[3] Some local residents even use it as a dumping place or call it a waste ground.
- It doesn't even have a name (although many years ago, it was known

as 'Gypsy's Acre' because of the travellers who habitually set up their camps on it). We have come to call it West Cross Common, but in the planning application it is simply labelled 'Land North of Chestnut Avenue'.

For all these reasons, it seems obvious the common would be vulnerable to development. And that is exactly what's happening.

The development has had the (no doubt unintended) consequence of galvanizing local people into forming a strong group in support of the common. Many concerned residents are now *paying attention* – turning up, writing letters, organising meetings, speaking to politicians, noticing birdsong, photographing insects, cataloguing, making lists, researching, inquiring, confirming, connecting and archiving. Many of them have been generous enough to share their knowledge and time with me for this book, and it is their efforts that have made it possible. I have included some of them in these pages.

Through their research, both in the field and in archives, they've found evidence for ancient drovers' routes still scored in the peat. Evidence suggests these could have been used 900 years ago by monks travelling from their Gower granges to the shore at Blackpill, where they would likely voyage across the bay to the mother house at Neath Abbey. In other places you can walk along old practice trenches dug before the First World War. As bracken has been cleared, springs and waterways have become more obvious, criss-crossing the land like blood vessels around a heart, and water is at the centre of the common's significance, particularly as we begin to face the challenges of climate change.

The common's shiniest gems, though, are natural. We are only a small group of enthusiasts, most armed with nothing more than smartphone apps to give us clues as to what we are hearing and seeing. But to date an astonishing 520 species have been found, including rare plants, fungi, birds and insects. Those little glimpses have led to conversations with a host of experts and academics, who have confirmed and verified sightings, and been impressed by the rich diversity here. They have written reports, submitted evidence, and the list of remarkable species continues to grow – a place where the uncommon is a common sight – hence the title of this book.

West Cross Common has emerged as a diverse mosaic landscape, a sequence of small and distinct habitats, fed by mineral-rich springs or ancient peat, with the ability to sustain a huge variety of plants and wildlife. Creatures that currently live happily on the common include adders, hedgehogs, jays, greenfinches, lizards – many on watch lists or with diminishing numbers as a result of the nature crisis. This packed-in variety of habitats is underpinned by a precious wet heathland system known as purple moorgrass and rush pasture. This habitat is usually designated when at least 12 indicator species are present – we have found 43 indicator species so far. It's a habitat-type now vanishingly rare worldwide thanks to human activity, and it is – apparently – a priority habitat in Wales, with a target of 'no loss'.[4] The marsh fritillary butterfly, which is noted nearby, and for which there is significant habitat on West Cross Common in the shape of its food plant, devil's-bit scabious, could recolonise this area. The marsh fritillary is an internationally protected species, and its habitats are also protected.[5]

The Welsh Government certainly knows how to talk the talk on priority habitats, with promises to protect it, and several schemes underway across Wales to revive heathlands that have been drained and dried out by closing up ditches and restoring the land to its natural wetland state.[6] By its own policymaking, the Welsh Government is also well aware that the loss of peat is disastrous as we fight to contain and store carbon and they also acknowledge peat's ability to store water, performing the role of a giant underground sponge that slowly releases rainfall into water courses so that nearby housing is not flooded by every heavy shower.

In this context you may be surprised that such a piece of land could ever be considered for 56 houses, more than 70 parking spaces, a road, and a substantial drainage and ditch system. Me too. But here we are. There is nothing we can do to reverse the planning consent that has already been granted on 'Land North of Chestnut Avenue' by Swansea City Council, but the battle is not over yet. The fact that this is common land – itself a special half-wild designation with ancient roots and long-held traditions of rights of access and use by the public – allows the common's future to hang by a thread, as the Welsh Government decides whether it should be de-registered. Their policy requires that there is no net loss of common land in Wales, so as part of the application a few acres of farmland in Murton, on the other side of the common, are offered in exchange in order that the houses can be built in West Cross.

Of course, none of us deny that affordable homes are needed. But we question why they must be sited on such rich, biodiverse land? What we would like to see instead is a better use of our existing housing stock, and of the brownfield sites that already exist. Even the poorer 'exchange land' would be preferable for housing than this wild and precious corner of the common. Possibly one of the reasons the common has come up on developers' radar is cost. It is often cheaper to build on greenfield than on other types of site.

But in a climate emergency, decisions about land use can't only come down to money. This is our moment to think differently about housing, to make necessary and possibly difficult decisions about how Wales can face climate change in a sustainable and positive way, for both people and planet. It requires radical planning policies from the Welsh Government, and we urgently need them to rise to the challenge.

If we really can't think beyond our own human interests, then let's remember that this area of common land sustains some of the most important species on the planet – pollinators. Without bees, butterflies, hoverflies, moths and beetles, there will be no crops, no plants, no salad, fruit, veg – in other words, no food. And therefore, no people.

I have written this book because I hope to give a voice to the unheeded – the common itself, the plants and animals that live on it, the residents who use it for their own health and wellbeing, and even to its history. The common has long been used by commoners in the legal sense, but also by 'common people', in a more informal sense – those who walk across it, exercise their dogs or horses, pick blackberries or other forageable crops, who rambled across it as children, the nature lovers who birdwatch or paddle or 'soodle'[7] their days away simply enjoying the space, solitude and quiet. By getting inside these people, creatures and plants I hope to sway some people to the common's side.

I also aim to create a record, albeit imperfect, of some of the flora, fauna and fungi that we've observed on West Cross Common. In doing so I am treading in the footsteps of many nature poets before me, but in particular those of John Clare, who himself lived through the Enclosure Act of 1807 and was broken-hearted by the resulting destruction of open commons, free countryside and rambling wildlife he'd so loved – 'that green for ever dear'. And when his beloved Helpston Green was destroyed he wrote:

> *Farewell delightful spot farewell*
> *Since every efforts vain*
> *All I can do is still to tell*
> *Of thy delightful plain.*

Clare is credited with being a poet of record as much as he was a nature or eco poet – and so in the same tradition I hope to capture what is so special about West Cross Common for future generations, placing it in a poetry jar of brine in case it is lost in the future, whether to housing, climate change or anything else.

I have come to love this common uncommon. It is a place my family goes to decompress, to explore, to learn. My older daughter has photographed it for her GCSE coursework, my younger daughter has been galvanised to write letters of objection to the development – perhaps a politically engaged citizen in the making. Future generations are being seeded.

The common has its moods. There are always new paths to try out, a shifting landscape dictated by the seasons, the weather, the water levels in the bog, and maybe even the common's own caprice. It is a special place, an understated, modest place, that seems so unlikely from the outside to hold treasures. And yet here it is, bristling with uncommonly rare gems.

---

[1]Planning Policy Wales, Edition 12, 2024
(https://www.gov.wales/sites/default/files/publications/2024-02/planning-policy-wales-edition-12_1.pdf); Swansea Local Development Plan 2010–2025
(https://www.swansea.gov.uk/media/5436/Swansea-LDP-2010-2025/pdf/adSwansea_Local_Development_Plan_2010-2025.pdf?m=1643721669737)
[2]See for example, 'Duke's trust's £281k for bridge', BBC, 7 January 2009
(http://news.bbc.co.uk/1/hi/wales/7815846.stm)

[3] See for example, 'Maintaining, Enhancing and Restoring the Peatlands of Wales: Unearthing the Challenges of Law and Sustainable Land Management', V. Jenkins and J. Walker, Journal of Environmental Law, 2022.

[4] *Wildlife Sites Guidance Wales: A Guide to Develop Local Wildlife Systems in Wales*, 2008 (https://www.biodiversitywales.org.uk/File/53/en-GB)

[5] Butterflies and the Law, UK Butterflies, (https://www.ukbutterflies.co.uk/webpage.php?name=law)

[6] 'Biodiversity Deep Dive prompts Welsh Government to triple peatland restoration in nature recovery promise', 2022 (https://www.gov.wales/biodiversity-deep-dive-prompts-welsh-government-triple-peatland-restoration-nature-recovery-promise)

[7] *Soodle* – linger, dawdle, saunter; a term used by John Clare

That green for ever dear

stand

and listen. just an old scrubby wasteland
nobody wants. bracken. bramble. armchair. ash.

no! stand. listen. there, gorse, blackened and reborn,
rib-tough. butter-yellow flowers mark spring.

hold my hand, and listen. linnets drift like seeds,
drown in their own sound, lift and fall, lightly out of brown.

close your eyes. listen. willow warblers and wrens,
unlit comets arcing between low trees, a blackbird's alarm.

just stop. breathe. listen. skylark, snipe, a grass snake's slide
through cotton grass. polecat. weasel. an otter's crunch.

& listen for the things you can't hear: bog asphodel, marsh fritillary,
orchid, marsh cinquefoil, bogbean, pipistrelle bat.

now. do you hear the plans rustle, how coins and glasses clink,
that distant thunder of diggers storming up the hill?

Commonplace

let me tell you the tale of this extraordinary ordinary.
this common everyday.
this rarity of ditches, bleached bracken
downtrodden by wind. stuck record of a song thrush
in that landmark thorntree.

this nation of roots, where uncommon wonders
are common as muck,
things you hardly see any more,
not since you were a child, but now
growing here, and there, and there:

early purple orchid, marsh willowherb,
buttercup, devil's-bit scabious, molinia, rush.
in motion – grasshoppers, chaffinches,
the blue flash of a jay's wing.
common things children have forgotten:
a ladybird on a finger,
a bullfinch's flute like a squeaking gate,
and a fox watching from the scrub,
wondering what unusual will happen next.

The common song

When I opened my mouth to sing, out tumbled a seed
And from the seed grew leaves, a stem, a flower

And from the flower came a scent, like musical notes
And the notes became wrens, scoring the summer

And the summer grew warm, like a lover's kiss
And the kiss became a ring, adorning my finger

And my fingers reached out, and found a gold-eyed magpie
And the magpie flew down, and brought me my lover.

Common nights

miniskirted and lipsticked,
night-time is when
she gathers her hemlines, her borders,
her taverns and bawdy houses.

in her dark clubs,
the patchwork quilt of star moss
and heathland are laid out on her waterbed:
wet buttonholes where craneflies & mosquito larvae rave.

she is fevered by lights.
the incessant beat. headlights and motorbikes,
straight lines on plans.

later, in darkness she feels safe enough to sleep.
water is a muscle barring trespassers,
keeping the council estate in its place. ivy is surveillance,
eavesdropping, spiking the martinis. unfooting
intruders in their shiny shoes.

at dawn, uncertain.
does she wake? are they real,
these willow warblers and bullfinches?
does she hallucinate fritillaries,
orchids, star-flowered asphodel?
sloomy figments of her common unconscious
surely too fabulous to be real.

Already he is a roar into her face

Fire, busy with his work,
unravels her, discards
what is not fastened in,
roasts her frogs and slow worms, strips
the soft herbs from her bones.

He reduces her to oil,
simmers her.
No more the cloth
of bracken and gorse
she had snatched up to cover herself,

and that song that was the air
suddenly blistered, stuffed,
swollen as a fist.

He has branded his name
deep into her heart.

Him she can live through.
But some trespasses
cannot be survived.

The common as a mother who is about to lose her children

she has that spider sense, her ganglions fused to the map
of each child's trundles and preoccupations
where the caterpillar gets her snack
or the violet her ditchwater drink.
she stocks the cupboard with their favourite things,
answers their calls, is there when
her goldfinch scaldies shriek open their mouths
for something anything please,
and when the hazelnuts ripen out of their vests,
when the jackdaws need breaking up,
when the badger rolls in from his nightshift.
Her arms are heavy with holding their coats,
listening to their stridulations,
she rolls her eyes when the teenagers
strut their magpie tails. She reads them bedtime stories,
howls lullabies over their empty stomachs,
encourages worms to come out from under the kerbs for air.
Soon they will take her children.
Each small parting is a torture on a torture,
an agony of helplessness, what no mother
should have to bear.

The common as a woman who is stretched too thin

Her diary is green and illegible, overgrown
with missed appointments.
Where has she been? Where is she expected?
Her history is bewildered,
her future double-booked.

Born from the confusion
of a charred egg, the milky way's blade
will fall any minute and spell her end.

Some things are certain.
Love. Laundry. Loss.
Perhaps she is beautiful.
Under her ferny blouse you can
follow deep lines with your fingertips. Ways men
forged, and children. Perhaps this
is her root. Her fate. Surrounded by open mouths,
always snagged somewhere on her own scarlines,
destined to keep running, running

into the scrawl of tomorrow's list,
where must her children be and who does she owe
and what's for dinner
and if she keeps on, she will find herself forced
flat on her back at the end of the long path,
where the ash tree fell, looking up at stars and
singing with her greenfinch heart:
I have been burned.
I am alive.

The common as an old woman
waiting at the bus stop

Never you worry I only wants to know
the green answers: when can I sprout
when can I unfurl when can I creep when can I twine
– these preoccupations of mine always ongoing green –
when can I leaf when can I bud when can I...?

this is how I goes on I'll talk to anyone.

sit by me, stargazer, *cwtch up*, *cariad*.
do you want an ivy cover for your sofa?
something sweet from my bag?
look up there, my dear,
like the wild pony.
It's only another pocked moon,
a friendly face in the tea-black sky.

A living autopsy of Clyne Common

Here we find splayed out the wide and green body
of Clyne, stone heavy on Gower's embalming table.
Drenching. Weeping black. All signs of undeath.
Gorse pinned raggedly to the breast.

Scars: one imaginary cul de sac. Heart a blackbird's nest.
Brain, a fox's den. All riverlets torn open, drowned.
Let us peel back turf. Cuticles of peat, pulsing,
warming their scales. Muscles an adder twist

of survival, steadied for winter's cold slab.
Blood solar-powered, a lizard broth. In the opened stomach,
the drink undrunk by ash trees, who fell last summer
and rested their collarbones in mud, past saving.

The head is Havisham veiled in a plastic bag.
There are signs of violence. Welts, blisters, a burn
across the soft midriff. Thigh abrasions, a finger-shaped
bruise. Someone wants to have their way with her.

But she's not done yet. See how the lungs still stutter
and swell, every cut fringed with new bindweed,
and here, when I part her ribs, how honeysuckle
springs up, how butterflies burst into life.

The common as a clockwork toad machine

When you find the key it is water,
which fits only this particular lock, crafted from peat.
Wind it. Set in motion the mainspring:
its pendulum swinging from
everlasting hibernation, to forever reborn.
The common is gilled. Its amphibian awareness
never sleeps. Without water it seizes.
Rain is the crank, the croaky ratchet,
waking the unconscious tadpole
in every dark pool.

It is beautiful – this sinking-back reduction of skin and innards
into the bog's mouth
    then later the miraculous re-emergence from soup,
burped out as black-specked jelly or fly's buzz.
Let it whir into motion, let it whizz.

Follow the suckers of this nonsensical map

where desire lines have been started
       by puddles and imagining and gaps between,
by grasses, holes in leaves, stunted stems
       above pockets in the earth, by necessity.

here, this kink in the path by a long-forgotten bramble
which grew in its crook, that hole by a mouse's quickline
       becoming a weasel's stalkline
becoming a fox's snoutline
       becoming a dogwalker's heartline.

that path by a stone kicked from place,
       nudged by a foal's stumble,
caught by a grass snake's weave,
       wetted by a passing cloud.

that road by a blade of grass bending,
       grazing a small chasm in dust,
where a dandelion seed blew in and settled,
       forced the earth apart with bone tongs,
made a shrew's shelter, which made a hunter's service station,
       which made a pavement for polecats,
which eased the way for the drovers,
       until the clock saw its potential
and drew it for us in stone.

Ask yourself what becomes of the lost

Clyne Common, Lockdown, 2020

If you hear a roar
it is only the sea's rush hour. The sigh
only the stream's inbox overflowing.
That shuffle, feathers doing their taxes,
this knock only a woodpecker delivering mail.

If they are anywhere surely they are in the starlings
springing airward together in a sudden start.
Or in the song thrush practising her voice.
Or in the robin busy embroidering his fire on ivy.

Bare branches, forlorn of their leaves,
stand black against sky. But birds are easier to see
in winter trees, and they are lively,
and singing, and look! The holly's leaves always forget to fall.

Instead she puts up her feast table for them.
There is green, and gloss,
and red, and splendour, and gold,
and here come the lost,
attending like kings in their feathers,
protected by her lovely thorns.

Common assumptions

Ych, it's all wasteland.
Bracken taken over,
all those furled-up fiddle heads in a tangle
so you can't see where you're going.
You can't get at the place. Worthless.
It gets into your coat, drenches you down to your skin.
It's a bog, a swamp, a nightmare. Quicksand.
Brambles worse than barbed wire.
There's nothing of any worth. A junkyard.
See where the kids have left
that old sofa, lit a fire, there by that old tyre swing,
that tipped-out den they made.
Commoners don't even use it for grazing.
No pannage these days, no estover. Nothing, no inkling, no coin.
Just those kids down there, looking for glow-worms,
remembering their way back into the blackbird's song.

Common questions

In the irregular shape
of the common's skylights
a conundrum of bats
zigzags an inquisition
on thin-boned leather wings:

how can you build here?
what is the appeal? how can I
wing? how can I soar? how can I reach?
how will I read their elevations?
navigate by lamplight?

what is this new development?
how will water be pulled up
by its roots? how will the camellia
feed me? how will the skylights open?
how will I...?

Welcome to the Museum of the Half-wild

Outside is a half-blue plaque. *This common*
belongs to the lord and manor, its
half-letters proclaim. The other half
is green, overgrown with ivy,
the words obscured, gnawed,
scratched out by claws. *This*
common is ours, it howls.

                You must
buy a half ticket, half price of course;
half the museum is free.

                The first
exhibit is a half-tyre swing,
dangling from an oak, half growing
through the wall, roots outside,
trunk breaking through. Mud
scuffs swirl half snail shells
beneath it on the half-tiled
floor.

             Next, half a contract,
half-signed by the king, transferring
ownership of the half-wild
museum to you. Half framed,
half written on the caravan wall.

                After that,
you can sit on the ripped half-sofa
– try it out! – an interactive display

with realistic smells (fox piss! old beer!
dog rose! puddle!).

There's half a
FOR SALE sign somewhere, and half
an artist's sketch of a twee street,
showing newly planted silver birch
(along one pavement only). Also half
a protest placard, half-heartedly
painted.

There's no set route, although
some paths are better than others.
Dress appropriately for the half weather.
Dogs are welcome (wild or tame, it's all
the same).

The museum half prides itself on its
accessibility. It is half open to all,
and of course, those with half membership
have special access – don't forget you have
estover, pannage and grazing rights!

Our history room is a must!
Discover how commons have always
been neither one thing nor the other:
wild, managed, owned, communal,
private, public and more!

Please take your rubbish home
with you. We may be called
a waste ground, but we don't half
offer great value.

The museum is a resource –
the community's battery pack! –
and so you may use it to recharge yourself
or your devices, and – we request – not
doing it by half.

           Please note: only one half
of the museum is open to the public.
The rest is in the process
of being sold to a housing developer.

Before you leave don't forget to cross
the bridge from an older way, and push
the green button, which holds us fast
to the wild, no matter how we pull away.

We thank you, half-heartedly, for visiting.

The uplifted ax no mercy yields

Sustainability

is key to our plans. Be assured
there are several schools nearby, including Catholic
and Welsh-medium primaries.

Our surveys tell us
the road network has capacity for additional cars
and public transport connections are excellent,
with several bus routes passing regularly.

There is capacity
at the two surgeries.
The local shops boast a chemist,
a post office, a café,
a sandwich shop, a hairdresser,
a chip shop, and a Chinese takeaway

plus, of course,
a general store selling anything
a person could need.

Sonnet for disturbed peat

Careful what you stir up. I've seen carbon spring from smoke,
take on breaths, try on a man's lungs for size.
Mad sculptor, carbon uses his dust to make, remake,
takes air and through pure will, solidifies.
Carbon fashions whole cities from fields,
conjures factories and chimneys from a crushed starling's song.
He copies bricks, cobbles, wheels,
landslips, slag heaps, looms; he eats the young.
I am but ash. Messenger between realms, tree father.
Slow-rooted, I account for the eggs and the pinecones.
I did not reckon on revolution. In the snap of a feather,
away went the crow, the skylark. Machines sprouted from bones.

More. Fast. Cheap. Still, we're all carbon-based.
And carbon wants to live. Never mind the cost. Never mind the waste.

Bog body

they said: you can certainly live
   where bog ends and house begins
      where ditch-drained gardens are fenced off
        where brambles are well-behaved
     where the pond can hold a whole flood.
but they forgot to mention she would become amphibian.

there's a breeze block underskin and concrete footings
yet still the bog leaks up into this house.
a wake-up call of toads crowds her windowsill
tadpoles swish past her patio doors.

     she can't sleep
for the gurgles and sloshings inside her walls
     as if her bedroom were a digestive tract
and there's always something trying to get inside her skin.

thirsting   she pads downstairs at night
squelches across carpets,
her cream rug sponging black
slips down the hill of the hall and into the tipped-over kitchen
the bog an architect with its own plans for her dormer
     a skew-whiff spirit level for the floors

this is how ancients were pickled in peat.
she lies, a nymph in the bath, looking up,
thanks the sun and moon for building her this house.
no matter the way it tips and croaks,
its corners dipped in black pools,
her teabag house on its rainstring.

you can grow accustomed to inky lines
along grouting, wicking up curtains
the tie-dye whitewash walls
the blackened fingernails, she thinks,
her hair in clots   eyes glazing   teeth bared
her flesh turning to fruit leather
& her toothbrush in its alabaster jar
                              her fridge with its salad bags
her favourite china bookend floating in frog soup:
everything will be preserved just as it is,
a warning for tomorrow.

When adder went to the shops

things happened he had not foreseen. To begin with
it took time to start his engine on such a cold day,
his heart slow as treacle. Once revved, he undulated
along pavements, shrew-quick, and was almost
at the corner when he found – annoyingly –
he'd forgotten his shopping bags. Mercifully, the parade
was not busy and somebody held open the door.
Inside the shop – rows of coloured foods in hard
containers. He eyed the tin openers.
The air bore the taste of chicken and snow.
He came eye to eye with a terrified mouse,
panting beneath the freezers. A seasoned sneak,
he was betrayed by the crunch of a prawn cocktail crisp
beneath his belly. They had run out of everything
on his list, except one shining herring jar, high out of his reach.
He approached the assistant but she fled, screaming.
Then his jaw vibrated with the thuds of many boots
as the queue of schoolchildren stampeded from the shop
and plastic-wrapped sweets rained in a clatter.
He yawned. Perhaps he could try the Chinese takeaway instead.
Alas, he realised. He had left his wallet in his other skin.

What we could learn from the study of absence

Kingfishers are unseen and unseen and unseen again
but remain unseen
a window opening on the river,
starting up sunlight as if it was birds, fleeting
out of the corner of your memory's eye
the airmail letter you didn't open.

Otters are a joke on the water
a reed bending down
to whisker the shape of otterback
the eyelash flutter of a fishturn
in the river's muscle, wanton splash of a duck's foot.

When they are not there, hares
lie panting like slices of moon on open fields
the road running across their middles
as though softness
was a story you read once
but can't remember how it ends.

Badgers are a bare skull in the woods;
a brainsize gap of earth
contains an unbristled heart
where the wind gathers
to huff down the bank's eye sockets.
You want to roll your eyeball down
just to see the grunt and claw
that made those gouges
but the dark is breathless and grieving.

List the absences: the lost, the missing. Soon
you will not be here to notice, either.
Your eyes closed on the world and hard, like coins
& I wonder if we will have learned anything.
No common, no fairwood, no Clyne.
Your green gone and the world lonely
and built of absences.

Spell of protection
A found poem, constructed of foraged fragments

From your flesh we summon strength for this spell:
courage from your leaves –
fern, bracken, tormentil, birdsfoot, ragwort, moss.

From your spine we summon resilience for this spell:
briar, charred gorse root, royal fern, oak,
creeping buttercup, thistle, bindweed, dock.

From your throat we summon seven breaths for this spell:
marsh fritillary, crow feather, thrush song,
dandelion seed, sneezewort, cottongrass, fly.

From your bones we summon timelessness for this spell:
rattling white galls, hazel, drovers' road, nettle,
bramble thorns, gorse spines, ancient black peat.

From your hips we summon energy for this spell:
wild rose, chestnut, bog asphodel, orchid,
pony, bedstraw, fox fur.

All these we press into your black dams.

we invoke your ancient name: *Clun* –
you are feminine, you are hip, you are thigh,
you are haunch, you are moor,
you are the ancient meadow.
With these tokens, we guard you,
With your name, we protect you.

Ryeground farm

Imagining a future in which 56 affordable eco-homes are built on the 'exchange land' at a farm on the other side of the common

These houses have it all. Reclaimed stone. Greywater systems.
Beautiful reciprocal roofs, each hand-carved, curved joist
resting on the next, like a circle of hands on shoulders.

Here, we can hold each other up. The windows gaze
over unbroken commons, wild horses and hollows filled
with still water. Sometimes the skies are oil paintings.

In the communal area there is the orchard where children
climb for apples. A greenhouse full of ripe tomatoes.
Someone turning soil for his next crop of onions.

You would never have believed you could afford it. Your own
solar panels, underfloor heating powered by the earth.
Money left over to buy a decent electric car.

You had forgotten how it felt to breathe clean air. To see
butterflies and bees in the garden, to wake to the clamour
of birdsong. Close to the good school, the doctor's surgery.

You are proud of what you helped build. That timber there,
that drystone wall. You have left your mark on these
houses. They have left their mark on you.

As are the changes of the green
So is the life of man

Susan

walks on storms.
If she could only pin it down
this land of turfy clouds
this weather system beneath her soles –
cumulous froths of fern with that glimpse
of upside palm. Held in a gust

she carries her own puddles
inside her boots, reaches beneath moss
to check the latest news, always
on the lookout with her bird alarm.

Rain sloshes in her coat pockets,
sphagnum moss roots in her heart.
Her blood is peat-black,
her hair a waterway.
More polecat than political,

I'm not really from here, she mutters
but there's something about the light –
I only want to save it.

Practice trenches

Lads like these have never been so soil-sore
digging themselves in. Have never
bid good day to the badger before,
with his forearms designed for the job.
It feels wrong, this opening up
of new wounds. Blisters on every palm.
Forming their flesh around shovel and spade,
becoming machine. Muscles and backs
and gangs and songs and a joke
to soothe the work. Soon they'll open
these arteries on French fields,
sleep in a crook of unfamiliar earth.
They'll give anything to be back here, then,
reliving these quiet trespasses into green.

The shard

Catch him on the right day and John's still there, age six, fetching
frogspawn with his sisters. A small traipse from Bellevue to the moor
ponds. He loved the way Woodland Avenue dwindled into the stream
& the steep hill slog of the bank. He made dens in bracken like a dog
circling, tramping it down, the fronds a ribcage, the boy a heart. He was
less interested in sky; soilformed. He wanted to find things tucked in
the pages of the earth: Second World War Nissen huts, Bronze Age
barrows, the monks' roads. Nobody for miles, just birdsong and lizards
and the cows munching summer verges. He is a living record of
forgotten farms, Upper Boarspit and Lower and Venn's and Grange,
where he trailed the milkman on his rounds, knees brown, 'til he was
dropped at the dairy to look around as he pleased. All long gone. You
can open him like a book, each leaf unfolding a layer of what came before
houses, before Gonhill and Bettsland and Cross Acre and Cedar,
the swallowed-up fields. He remembers Moorside Road being taken by
its scruff and shaken 'til it stood stiff over the water. The smell of wet
peat, beetles gleaming under stone. What is left is shard, a splinter of
what was there before, artefact, emblem, the place where a line must
be drawn, a reminder of the dear and ancient green.

Acre's last gypsy

4.47am turn of some century
Mrs Hearn neither awake nor dreaming,
is starving for constellations.
She reclines on her ivy couch
right on the high street of moorgrass,
'til she huffs both feet into breezy rushes
steam in her mouth,
threads her broken laces through stars
(plough shape, bear shape) and goats
out to pour dawn into vicar's tea.

She always visits in her black
handmedown trilby, seenbetterdays boots.
An early riser, vicar serves daily
her favourite biscuits:
a square trade for skylark eggs.

Eveningtime she packs her pipe
with sand dunes,
loves the slither of smoke
uptide and around moon.
Takes her tobacco for a solitude.

In her last hours on the ward, she'll croak:
take me outside to die under sky.
And they will,
her boots left behind, leaf cold.
One less mouth for the stars to feed.

The Dictionary of Plants

Carol is the archivist of dells and glades,
the drovers' roads, her eye tuned to wonder.

Her frequency ferned, she is green-hair-streak-winged, her brain
a tabulation of hummocks and tussocks, ditches
and dor bug gatherings. She is a glass slide

of locations, a gathering of stems pulled
inwards and held at the centre, each seed head
a card in her index. It is as if she
carries her girlhood inside, can magic

things into being: those gorse shield bugs
at their tea parties, sweet motherbugs
fatherbugs and childbugs
set around their yellow tablecloth,
which set her off wondering about birds
who gather to gorse: then – ah!
that Dartford warbler appears
with his red napkin tucked beneath his chin,
she adds another character to her wondrous tally.

Drovers

Each journey begins with prayer.
Like water they flow from grange to shore;
Like bees with their honeycombs of beer;
Like sheep they are tightly bonded;
Like geese they deny their fate;
Like muddy boots they choose a liquid path;
Like rain their route changes;
Like cartwheels they bear their verses;
Like the mother house they welcome travellers;
Like the moorings they are tethered;
Like firewood they sleep along the way;
Like oars they love the sea;
Like a homecoming they carry their load;
Like the road they leave their mark;
Like their prayers they will take a different path home.

A warlord of ecology

Mike stands on this battlefield
and knows its trenches –
he is infantry,
a shoulder-cocked scout,
marching, his spyglass
raised to fern.

Seasoned, he studies the lie
of the land, says they don't stand
an earthly, has tramped his way
through every campaign,
charged down bulldozers,
besieged meads, skirmished at meanders.

Mike has held the line, moved
the front, weathered.
Seen too many poppies sprout
on hard shoulders. Victory-
scarred, loss-torn, he always
responds to the call.

Hazel The Dog

I am let loose –
snipped from the hand
and running
pelting into smells
soil on my belly
the creatures leave
trails behind
fragments
of their chemistry
woven like thread
around fernstems

I am unstoppable –
my nose a knife
cutting through paragraphs
of gorse I know what happened here
it was dark
the dirt rose up
out of itself
ate a nut
curled outwards
became a heart
wrapped in fur
screeched under the owl's claw

I can hunt
chase pieces of story
along their own lines
pant and try the air
under wings

but there isn't enough squirrel
I would prefer the story
to always end with squirrel

Laura

The best time of day for birdsong
is first light. I'll tell you how I started.

It was crystal therapy. Or meditation. Or fate.
Or my sunk heart. I was hauled in

to this shipwreck land. I came here once.
But this place. It put its spores in me. This bad

land. This gorgeous curse of moss and birds and
birdsong and lists of calling birds.

A parasite in my head. Every elsewhere I listened
was library hushed compared with the orchestra

of this place. It pinned me down. Stitched a sampler
of feathers across my skin. I knew where greenfinches

spent their days, where black caps. I tuned my bird mind. If only
these blooms had more light. There were days I did not know

if I would make it home I was an artist painting my piles
of brash. I learned hedgehog and moth and solitude

and I was hermit. I learned grass snakes lay their eggs
in rotting vegetation and next year I will spread out warm bracken

for them. I am custodian, browser, here will be a river of flowers,
here the yellow wagtails come, here red campion, here

marsh cinquefoil but if we let the bracken grow around the birch
it is a funeral pyre, a tinderbox, ready to go up.

It's like this special mosaic of habitats every hundred yards or so,
the birds that aren't afraid when you are on your own.

I had been craving greenwild my whole life until everything
led me here. The Chinese sign of the wild boar. Fate. Meditation.

I have become myself. Keystone. Rootling up bare soil
around the scabious, earth engineer, so next year more will grow.

Sweet it was to mark the flower

Dandelion

so blow the dandelion clock.
your time is almost out.
geese are overhead,
swallows taken flight.
summer is ending,
we saw her last sun pass.
the first oak leaf has
dandled down to grass.
please, blow your clock,
and set free next summer's seeds:
so our wild uncommon places
can feed tomorrow's bees.

Black cap visits

Welcome, migrant, with your smart grey suit and mourner's cap.
You landed on the gutter of our grief and bowed your respects.

Your keen eye, your quick wing reminds me of those doomed flutters.
And black cap, with your wedding suit, you will soon leave us too,

your migrations laced into your heart. You are restless, called away,
you know how to throw yourself upwards into a storm.

Imagine you, still. No flutter of pulse on the ultrasonic black screen.
You with your mourner's cap, searching for home. Tumbled into black.

Sometimes I think I hear you in the hazel tree. I want to know.
Did you find it? Did you find your answer to the question of home?

I have two daughters now. They like to fill the bird feeder.
And your lover was here, in her brown hat. I saw her pause. Settle.

Tormentil

crowd of children
leaves a-chatter
tumble in the mire
not quite buttercups
sunny faces run
amok stronger than
their tiny size run
along look at how they
soodle their games
across the pathways
hopscotch groundcover
run all about
midge-giddy
in their
growing up little
heliographs of joy

Wild angelica

came creeping from the woods one day
out into light
liked what she saw   got comfortable
in the lane drank up all the sunshine
meandered along
found the wild hedge
listened to the sparrows' gossip
liked what she heard   got eager
for adventure shook out her hair
let the wind blow her
seeds and all
up to the wild moor
set down her roots in ancient earth
liked what she tasted   got strong

then rain came

found herself unfolding
telescoping ribs up umbrella flower
drew a crowd.
liked what she could do. made herself
open   spread out.
splendid pavilion for the hoverflies.

Golden-ringed dragonfly

fly backwards, you living light
into the eye of the river
dab your eggs in her blanket folds

or forwards, you darning needle
into the blind leaf
stitch the crowds of midges

or up, you enamel pin
into the lid-darned dazzled sky
distract these common thieves

or down, you toothed copter
into the beating earth
seed a few more of your sycamore wings

Earthball

Don't disturb warty potato.
He is hard at his concentration.
He is chewing up mouthfuls of soil,
composting, making them into bloat.
He is at his important work, his deskjob,
with his mouth deep in the coffee cup,
stewing, turning his insides black.
He is all scales, putting on weight.
Don't mind him, his deadline
is the next shower of rain.

Riddle
Aur dan yr eithin

What am I? You'll never find me in the furze maze,
my laugh hung out like laundry on the spikes.
I'm always ahead of you, the spines
spring back, settle in their place,
a drop of sky trembles on the thorn.
I like to win. Yellow is for hope and you might
easily get snagged up on cowardice, get
stuck in, but this phoenix plant is greased,
sharp for firing rebirth.
I can make bread as easily as death.
If you want a clue:
don't fall for bracken's silver, don't starve
in the heather. I like to lie on my gold bed,
and you can only kiss me when
my flowers are in flood.

devil's-bit scabious

starts in earth with a dream about flying:
seed with ideas above your station.

you watch caterpillars transform
into living bean-pods; emerge with stained

glass wings twitching into air, then unhitch
into sky. you hoist your kite string with its purple sail

and all intentions to fly. you are beautiful.
butterfly clouds gather, pollen-suckers with their easy

pennons, flags aflutter, fritillaries and hoverflies,
you strain your spine for their aerofoil glamour

you are cocked, muster every feather
of your flowers. wish for a surge of wind to lift you

but you cannot take to air.
devil's got your roots between his teeth.

Polecat

slinks, like a chain
with his sly links sliding
through articulate grasses
a slice of moon balanced on his nose:
sudden clip of night on an unsuspecting bone
he is a graceful last chapter in an unravelling life
a coiling uncoil of spine from a hole furred
and underfurred and almost purple
like one of those clouds that
promises rain and then
unveils morningstar.

Sneezewort

sways inside-out as though
a wind exploded through her bloomers
she'll kill or cure, white tansy,
not so pure, but heroic when pressed to heel.
look at her, on parade,
she lines the lane to the children's home,
gawking at memories. it's where
little girls picked nosegays
for brand-new mothers
where left-behind boys dried
their tears on nurse's apron.
now indestructible
tardigrades itch the
watermoss at her feet,
wild ponies snort and huff,
foalmad, funnelwebs
wind their grey
handkerchiefs round stems,
spillages of dew
caught trembling between

Royal fern

there is a regal man
standing with his feet in the ditch
nodding his head to all the other ferns:
good morning, crowded fiddle heads,
do you like my flower spears?
do you like my pinnate crown?
do you like my gilded spore tips?
do you like my rusty wig?
will you bow your ferny stems
to see my ancient roots?
don't mind my wet shoes
I am only king osmund the waterman
dining on bog onion
for a hundred years
while I wait for my audience

Purple moor grass

He spent years holding it together –
thatch over the soil ghetto,
weeping his bruises up his arms,
feeling around in the dark,

rooting for another tomorrow.
Hair cropped short
focused on personal growth
just one more shot won't harm.

Always more at home in the drink,
he sometimes feels he's drowning.
A long dry spell wouldn't go amiss,
but he'd rather that cool first sup

that gurgle of a fresh pour. It feels
so good to lay your head down
on this soft flank of earth, sighing,
dissolving into liquor.

Purple loosestrife

After John Clare

Long purple lofts up his ungainly crane
all confidence, constructs his square column –
There! You see, it is long purple again.
How he loves to cobble up each totem.

So he bides his days at the blea-pond edge
to scheme and plot his best waterside views,
then bulldozes over the hapless sedge
and oh, how his purple accrues.

Leaf over leaf, his shady roof is built,
So his flowry castle arises.
And skyscraper tall, and hardly a-tilt
a flies' hi-rise des-res he devises.

Scrap Bracken / A Drowning

A thousand-lensed eye marches up the hill
waving its curled lashes.
Incessant. They used it as evidence
for the scrap value of this place.
This green ocean, drowning itself.

Commoners once cropped bracken
for ovens
for bread
for beds
for soap
for sciatica
for smoking
for animal feed
for fertiliser
for glass.

Bracken carries an alphabet, bears a cross,
can write a letter to heavens, or devils.
It stores ancient powers:
makes the snake invisible,
brings God to the stonechat,
eternal youth to the toad,
keeps witches from lizards.

To those who damage its fronds:
bracken keeps watch.
Beware its poisoners' habit.
Beware the green tide, rising.

Bogbean

Have you met
this wayward mudlark?
This spring ethereal bean
who spends most months
with her head buried
in bog, but rises
with buds pink and mole
snouted, to blink into May.
Look what treasures she
has found! – her hairy flowers
thrust into bees' beards.
Here she is, star flowered
but unshaven, a blind whiskery
woman with white hair shining,
and the broadest, kidney grin,
pointing out her peat stalls
and welcoming us in.

Marsh fritillary

your wings are an unintentional heat map
of your demise
more patterned than other fritillaries
a stirring mosaic
where white means no sightings
yellow very few
orange a handful
red more than ten

return, so we can glimpse you
warming yourself on devil's-bit
a scorch against the clouds

Adder

is utter sundappled boulder defender
ratter, weak-eater,
heat-addicted heather adorner
solar-adorer,
many-headed hydra,
daughter, dam,
dwindling incubator,
stolen egg aider and abetter,
heart-shatterer,
mouse didderer,
gorse beader,
ladder-backed spine-leader,
bronzed-header,
sometime buzzard fodder,
curled-up battery charger,
jewelled dowel-rod,
hunted predator,
admired elder,
common awe-adder,
and this is adder's *adre*.

Bog waxcap

when you went missing
we released a list of your distinctive features:
waxy hat, red
strawberry birthmark,
diminutive,
one scarlet limb,
gills, fans, hairs,
your red umbrella.

but what makes you tick? they asked.
you like to put up your umbrella in the rain
and digest the dissolved organic
matter of the world, we replied.

we supplied the full list of 148 places
you had been known to frequent.
they searched them all.
but we know where you ended up:
under the patio.

bone-breaker

you are a blonde star flower at the lectern,
with so much to say.
you are a cluster of rhetorical sunlights,
bog asphodel: an optimistic fistful of yellow leaflets
each one packed with information:

here read about soil!
here read about creeping rhizomes!
here read about peat!
here read about rare moths!
about wet heathland and ancient seedbanks!

you are a protest
placard, your neon blazoning,
a yell in the green,
you have deep-rooted reasons
for believing in your cause.
your petals are a fringed meeting.
you are a punch in the eye,
phosphene bright.

you are known for breaking bones
slim spike busting from
the bruised socket.
you can break anything:
ground, hearts, silence.

Marsh violet

with her head very low downcast
among grasses, not a penny to rub together
lifts herself out of her roots and dips her feet
in water like a pen in ink. Ready.

Memoirist of the forgotten, she scores her work
on her own face with a bruise-black nib. Asks
a nearby snowdrop if every new sheet
could be laundered petal white.
Each body washed and healed,
miraculous.

She could write an elegy in her own blood
for the common people who've worked this land.
It would say brave, tough, hardy, clever.
It would remember how each one grew
from the dirt, strained upward to catch the light.

Jays in love

I heard the jays a-murmuring, a-murmuring their love
up in the sycamores, a-murmuring their love

I have never heard the like of it, a-murmuring they were
close murmurs of the senses, intimate and pure

a-murmuring like flower sounds, & the forest evergrowing
a-murmuring like hearts they were, their wing feathers singing

I tried to learn their lyrics, but their sweet bird-voices
forgot their screams and sabres, and were liquid in their phrases

they murmured of the fields, they had lately greenly seeded
they murmured of the trees, and the woods they had created

they murmured of their love, and in their murmured cries
was their love of the green wilds, and the everlasting skies

Notes

A number of references are made to works by John Clare, including a stanza in the introduction, and the section headers, which are all from his poem 'Helpston Green', apart from 'Sweet it was to mark the flower' which is from his poem 'Reccolections [sic] after a Ramble'. These and all other references to Clare herein are taken from *John Clare: Major Works* (Oxford World's Classics, 2008) edited by Eric Robinson and David Powell.

The law locks up the man or woman: Extract from 'The Goose and the Common', an anonymous poem about 18th-century enclosures of commons.

Common nights:
sloomy – a word used by John Clare to mean slow, dreamy.

The common as an old woman waiting at the bus stop:
cwtch – to cuddle; *cariad* – love, dear.

Common assumptions:
pannage – the commoners' right to let their pigs forage e.g. for acorns; *estover* – the commoners' right to gather firewood.

Spell of protection:
Clun – 'Clyne' in Welsh, also the Welsh feminine noun for hip, thigh, haunch, moor and meadow.

Acre's last gypsy: This poem is inspired by memories shared on the website 'A History of Mumbles': https://sites.google.com/site/ahistoryofmumbles/your-memories/so-what-did-we-do-for-kicks-by-anne-ardouin-nee-wilkinson

Sweet it was to mark the flower: For an area to be considered species rich, and worthy of designation as a priority habitat such as 'purple moorgrass and rush pasture', 12 indicator plant species must be observed from a given list. To date, naturalists have recorded 43 such species at West Cross. Those included in this book are noted here. There is also protected habitat of the marsh fritillary butterfly in the shape of devil's-bit scabious.

Tormentil: indicator species *Potentilla erecta*. *Soodle* – John Clare's word, meaning linger, dawdle, saunter.

Wild angelica: indicator species *Angelica sylvestris*.

Riddle:
Aur dan yr eithin – taken from the Welsh proverb '*Aur dan yr eithin, arian dan y rhedyn, newyn dan y grug*' – gold under the gorse, silver under the bracken, starvation under the heather, referring to the quality of soil, and therefore the value of the land, found under the three plants. The solution to the riddle is gorse.

devil's-bit scabious: indicator species *Succisa pratensis* and also the protected habitat of the marsh fritillary butterfly.

Sneezewort: indicator species *Achillea ptarmica*.

Royal fern: indicator species *Osmunda regalis*.

Purple moorgrass: indicator species *Molinia caerulea*.

Purple loosestrife: indicator species *Lythrum salicaria*. John Clare called these flowers 'long purples'. *Blea* is his word, meaning bleak, exposed or wild; *flowry* is his spelling of flowery.

Bogbean: indicator species *Menyanthes trifoliata*.

Marsh fritillary: indicator species *Euphydras aurinia*.

Adder:
Adre – home.

Bog waxcap: The 148 places mentioned in the poem refer to the number of recorded UK sightings of the species *Hygrocybe coccineocrenata* on the National Biodiversity Network (NBN) Atlas website. Many waxcaps are now considered rare or threatened.

Bog asphodel: indicator species *Narthecium ossifragum.*

Marsh violet: indicator species *viola palustris.*

Further reading

Common Land in Britain: A History from the Middle Ages to the Present Day, Angus J. L. Winchester (Boydell Press, 2022).

Report on the character and condition of West Cross Common, Swansea, Clive Chatters, 2023, commissioned by The Gower Society.

Acknowledgements

First, my thanks and admiration to the many members of the West Cross Common campaign, who work tirelessly in their efforts to save the common from development. Particular thanks go to those who spared time to be interviewed for inclusion in these pages: Susan Cole, Carol Crafer, Mike Crafer, Laura Sheldon and local historian John Powell. Thanks too for additional help and advice from wildlife experts Dr Dan Forman and Neil Jones.

I would like to give my thanks to Maggie Blewitt, Jean James and Lesley Williams for their continued friendship, support and feedback on my poetry; and likewise to the Salty Poets – Emily Vanderploeg, Mari Ellis Dunning, Rhys Owain Williams, Natalie Ann Holborow, Al Kellerman and Adam Silman. Also thanks to Glyn Edwards and fellow learners at the Poetry School for their helpful comments on a poem in progress.

Once again, Susie Wildsmith's editing has been beyond brilliant, so enormous thanks to her, and of course to the whole team at Parthian.

Finally, my everlasting thanks to my family, my husband Phil and daughters Gwennan and Mabli; my parents Joy and Meirion; my sister Jo and her family – for their love, encouragement and support.

PARTHIAN *Poetry*

The language of bees
Rae Howells

ISBN 978-1-913640-69-9

£9.00 | Paperback

'Rae Howells forges a unique and sparkling language, which is capable of giving us all the wonder and richness, the multisensual onslaught, of the world around us.'
– Jonathan Edwards

How can we have hope in a world that is dying? With a forensic eye, Howells takes us on a journey through ordinary human lives and the extraordinary natural world we are in danger of losing.

Moon Jellyfish Can Barely Swim
Ness Owen

ISBN 978-1-913640-97-2

£10.00 | Paperback

'Form and feeling combine to create a collection which rewards the reader with a mesmerising portrait of a much-loved landscape brimming with startling imagery.'
– Samantha Wynne-Rhydderch

Moon jellyfish live a life adrift. Owen's second collection explores what it is to subsist with whatever the tides bring. Poems that journey from family to politics, womanhood and language.

PARTHIAN *Poetry*

Wild Cherry: Selected Poems
Nigel Jenkins

ISBN 978-1-914595-22-6
£10.00 | Paperback

'He became the unacknowledged national poet of his generation, an open-hearted soul whose poems embodied much of what our nation is today – diverse, passionate, tender and unafraid to take a hard look at its political and cultural complexity.'
– Menna Elfyn

'Nigel Jenkins has a staggering presence in the literature of Wales. His poetry was both political and beautiful, deeply human, wonderfully cosmological and often scathingly humorous. Swansea's most amiable bard and, undoubtedly, its most popular poet since Dylan Thomas.'
– Tôpher Mills

Hymnal
Julia Bell

ISBN 978-1-914595-11-0
£10.00 | Paperback

'Moving, tender writing with a haunting evocation of place and time.'
– Hannah Lowe

Visiting Aberaeron in the 1960s, Bell's father heard a voice directing him to minister to the Welsh. This unique memoir in verse tells a story of religion, sexuality and family.